Blessings and Invocations

For Everyday Life

Rose Alba and Penny Barham

Blessings and Invocations

For Everyday Life

Rose Alba

&

Penny Barham

Illustrated by

Angela Davis

Hubbardston, Massachusetts

Asphodel Press
12 Simond Hill Road
Hubbardston, MA 01452

Blessings and Invocations for Everyday Life
ISBN 978-0-6152-3791-6

Printed in cooperation with
Lulu Enterprises, Inc.
860 Aviation Parkway, Suite 300
Morrisville, NC 27560

To the chief blessings of my life:
my husband Leslie
and my daughters Morgana and Pip.

—Rose Alba

I have been blessed with many friends and a wonderful family;
This book is especially dedicated to my mother and father, my sons Joe and
Luke, and my grandchildren Frank and Maggie.

I also dedicate this book to my dear friend Asphodel, who has passed on.
Without her I would never have had the confidence or courage to put my
ideas and beliefs into writing.

—Penny Barham

Contents

Introduction: The Spirit In Everyday Life .... *i*

Part 1: Daily Blessings

The Days of the Week 1

Sunday – Invocation to the Sun 3

Monday – Invocations to the Moon 5

Tuesday – Invocation to Mars 11

Wednesday – Invocation to Mercury 13

Thursday – Invocation to Jupiter 15

Friday – Invocation to Venus 17

Saturday – Invocation to Saturn 19

Part 2: Hearth and Home

Blessings for the Home 24

Blessing for the Threshold 24

Blessing for the Hearth 25

Blessing for the Kitchen 26

Blessings for the Bedrooms 28

Blessing for the Study 29

Blessing for the Bathroom 30

Blessing for the Garden 31

Blessing for an Altar or Sacred Space 32

Part 3: The Season Round

The Wheel of the Year 36

A Blessing at the Winter Solstice 38

A Blessing at Imbolc (Candlemas) 40

A Blessing at the Spring Equinox 41

A Blessing at Beltane (May Day) 43

A Blessing at the Summer Solstice 44

A Blessing at Lammas (Lughnnasadh) 46

A Blessing at the Autumn Equinox 47

A Blessing at Samhain (Halloween) 49

Part 4: Invocations for Special Occasions

Blessings and Invocations for Special Occasions 52

Invocation for a Naming Ceremony............................ 52

Blessing for a Naming Ceremony 53

Blessing for a New Mother 53

Blessing for a New Father 54

Blessing for a New Parent or Guardian 54

Menarche Blessing for a Young Woman................... 56

Blessing for a Young Man.. 57

Blessing for a Commitment Ceremony...................... 57

Asphodel's Poem for a Commitment Ceremony 58

Blessing for Work... 59

A Welcome to Cronehood 60

A Welcome to Retirement.. 60

A Blessing at the End of Life..................................... 61

Final Blessing at Asphodel's Funeral 62

Part 5: Gods and Spirits

Invocations to Deities 66

The Scorpion... 67

In Honour of Yemaya 67

To Oya... 68

To Bride... 68

To Sulis.. 69

To Epona 69

To Kuan Yin... 70

Invocation to Sekhmet... 71

To The Horned One 72

To The Holly King... 73

A Lament For Thammuz 75

Invocations to Animals.. 76

Introduction: The Spirit In Everyday Life

This book is for people who are looking to bring the sacred into their everyday life and who may not know quite where to start. It could also be useful to the more seasoned traveller who is looking for fresh ideas. It celebrates the meeting of the mundane and the spirit, and the bringing of spirit into our everyday life, which is important if we are to make our journey on this Earth a sacred one.

Many of us are brought up with the idea that "blessings" can only be conferred, and "invocations" (formal salutations to or calling on a Deity) can only be made, by certain people: priests, ministers of religion, special people who have been dedicated to a higher source, and who are sometimes seen as above or set apart from the ordinary lives of everyday folk. Blessings, prayers and invocations come under the sphere of "religion", and "religion" is something that happens only on a particular day of the week or at certain events and festivals.

In this book you will certainly find ways to honour and celebrate special events and festivals, but you will also find ways to celebrate every day of the week, and to honour every room of the house. Most importantly, these blessings and invocations can be used by the ordinary person; no particular spiritual or academic qualifications are needed, and it is not necessary to be a member or any particular belief system. The festivals celebrated in the Wheel of the Year, and the Gods and Goddesses saluted in the invocations, are certainly "pagan" festivals and "pagan" Gods, in the widest sense of the word "pagan"[1] — the beliefs of the ordinary people who lived on the land, as opposed to the hierarchical, structured religious system imposed by those in power. This means you! All you need is an open mind, the belief that you can find the sacred in every area of life, and the acceptance that the Divine can be revealed in many aspects and under many names.

Although we have divided the book into sections, this is just to make it easier for the reader to find their way around. In fact,

---

[1] From the Latin *paganus* , a villager or rustic person.

everything is connected and there will be overlaps. Some of the sections can be used every day; for example, the invocations for the days of the week. The section on the Wheel of the Year has a definite form and it is clear when to use it. However, there will also be particular events and special occasions in our lives which we may want to mark with a blessing or invocation, especially those of us who are outside of organised religions. This book covers these areas as well. Naming ceremonies for babies, coming-of-age celebrations, commitment ceremonies, marking our transition into old age and funerals are all important events that we may want to mark as sacred. We have also included a section on Blessings for the Home which may be particularly useful when moving into a new home, or if something unpleasant has happened, such as a burglary.

There will be times when we are especially in need of help. Animals have particular powers that we may wish to tap into for this purpose—traditionally, human beings have done this since ancient times. The section on animals is far from a definitive list, but we hope it gives the reader an idea of what is possible and we encourage them to search out animals that are especially important to them. The section on invocations to Deities expands upon the list of "classical" Deities associated with the days of the week, but again only provides examples and represents a handful of the boundless possibilities.

This book does not provide a dogma. We hope it encourages and inspires the reader as they walk their individual path, and provides a resource and a place to begin.

PENNY BARHAM AND ROSA ALBA
2008

Part 1:

Daily Blessings

The Days of the Week

Have you ever wondered why and how the days of the week were named? The seven-day week was adopted by the Roman calendar in 321 C.E., although it is certainly older than that, and is thought to have originated in Ancient Mesopotamia. The Romans named the seven days after the Seven Celestial Bodies—the Sun, the Moon, and the planets Mars, Mercury, Jupiter, Venus and Saturn. Remember that in ancient times it was thought that all of these revolved around the Earth, and the outer planets of our Solar System had not yet been identified, so the days of the week were thought to be symbolic of cosmic harmony and coherence.

Of course, the Seven Celestial Bodies were also worshipped across the ancient world as Deities, and so each day was seen as being under the auspices of the God or Goddess after whom it was named. Thus it was not only suitable to honour a Deity on his or her particular day, but also to deal on that day with those tasks, decisions or areas of life which that Deity oversaw.

This custom persisted even into Christian times, when planetary influences, rather than the blessings of a divinity, were assigned to each day. Nowadays, many people are rediscovering a relationship with the old Gods, and there is a general realisation that the Divine has many aspects.

Whether you prefer to think in terms of planetary influences or divine intervention, you may like to honour each day of the week with a short invocation to focus your mind upon the energies most closely in tune with that day. You will find that this not only enables you to concentrate upon the present without becoming overwhelmed by the demands of the week, but that it also helps you to appreciate each day as a gift from the Universe, an opportunity to enhance and enrich your life and your spiritual journey.

In Latin, the days of the week were named as follows: Dies Solis, Dies Lunae, Dies Martis, Dies Mercurii, Dies Jovis, Dies Veneris, and Dies Saturni. In French, Italian and Spanish one can easily identify these Roman names, but the English language has Anglo-Saxon roots as well, and we have substituted Teutonic equivalents for four of the Roman Gods: Tiw or Tyr, God of War, replaces Mars, giving us Tuesday; Woden, God of Wisdom, replaces Mercury, giving us Wednesday; Thor, the Thunder God, replaces Jupiter, giving us Thursday; and Freya, Goddess of Love and Fertility, replaces Venus, giving us Friday.

In the following invocations, I have referred to the Gods by their Roman names since these are also the names of the planets, but if the Norse names, or any other equivalent feel more familiar for you, there is no reason why you should not use those instead. Enjoy your week, and replenish your spirit with blessings for each new day!

Sunday – Invocation to the Sun
Sol Invictus, the Unconquered Sun

Hail, Sol Invictus,
Son of the Universe,
Light of the World,
Bright Charioteer,
Beloved Sun!

Lord of the Dance,
Lover of the Earth,
Ripener of Seed,
Bringer of Joy!

Light of the Moon,
Warmth of the Sea,
Father of all life on Earth,
I call upon Thee!

Child of Winter,
Lover of Spring,
Husband of Summer,
Father of Autumn,
I call upon Thee!

This invocation may be used to honour and invoke the Sun's energy on the first day of the week. It does us all good to remember that life on this planet was born from the interaction of sunlight upon water, and that the star which sustains our solar system is indeed literally the father of all the children of Mother Earth. This is the day to appreciate your life!

Although there have been solar goddesses in some cultures—for example, Amaterasu in Japan and Sunna in Scandinavia—in the Graeco-Roman tradition which we are using here, the Sun has been mostly identified with male polar energy, the generator rather than the birth-giver of life, the symbolic and alchemical opposite of the female energy associated with the Moon, the Earth and the Sea.

The Sun blesses us with healing and illumination, strength of the conscious mind, the growth and progress of ideas and projects, physical strength and well-being, and the nurturing and growth of children. He is also associated with fatherhood and male potency, so this is a good day to spend time with your father, or if you are a father, with your children. It is also a good time to ask for illumination on that search for the perfect lover, but beware of getting burned! Respect the Sun's power, and don't let yourself become dazzled or blinded!

Light one gold or yellow candle, burn Frankincense, display some sunflowers, cornflowers, poppies or marigolds, wear gold, red or yellow, and invite the sunshine into your life. Meditate upon the miracle of life, the cycle of the seasons and of seed and harvest, the beauty of Mother Earth as she responds to the Sun's warm caress and brings forth bud, flower and fruit. Ask for the past to be healed, the present illuminated, and the future made warm and welcoming for yourself and your loved ones. Give thanks for your life, both physical and spiritual, and bask in the Sun's love!

Monday – Invocations to the Moon

Monday—moon-day—is traditionally associated with the Moon, but of course it may fall at any stage of the lunar month, and it is important to be aware of the Moon's phase when approaching or meditating upon her. I have therefore included four different invocations, which may also be used to connect with the Moon as she enters each new phase, irrespective of the day on which it falls.

The monthly cycle of the Moon's changing shape—from the slim silver crescent of the New Moon, visible at sunset, to the full, round Queen of the Night, and finally to the white husk of the waning crescent which lingers in the morning sky—has always been linked to the monthly cycle of women. The Moon rules the unconscious mind, as the Sun rules the conscious. She is associated with intuition and subtle influence—female territory. But the ebb and flow of the tides, caused by the Moon's gravity, is mirrored not only in the menstrual flow, but also in the ebb and surge of fluid within all living things—for are we not all, according to science, seventy per cent water? Thus men as well as women experience a monthly cycle ruled by the Moon, even if the signs of it are less obvious.

Invocation to the New Moon

Hail, Bright Sister,
Virgin of the Evening Sky,
Lady of Beginnings,
Bringer of dreams and of possibilities!
May my new beginnings take root under your protection;
May my hopes and my dreams unfold to your light!

You may make this invocation whenever you see the slim right-handed crescent of the New Moon in the evening sky. Each month she brings a new start, a clean slate, a whole new set of possibilities into our lives. As the Moon waxes in the sky, from new to full, so beginnings become progress, possibilities become reality, and hopefully dreams may

come true. Matters may arise from the unconscious into full
consciousness, desire may grow in intensity, and inner promptings may
become more urgent.

When the Moon is new, light two new white candles, display white
flowers (preferably in bud), wear something clean and white. Burn any
incense with a sweet, light aroma that pleases and inspires you. Take
particular note of your dreams, hunches and intuitions, and meditate
quietly upon them. Let the seeds of your future arise from your
unconscious and take root in reality, ready to blossom in your life as
the month progresses. Ask for help with any new projects, tasks or
challenges that face you, and ask the bright young Moon to bless your
children, or any young people in your care, with hope, healing and
happiness as they grow.

Invocation to the Full Moon

Hail, Bright Lady,
Queen of the Night Sky,
Mother of Mystery,
Ship of the Night!
Light of the Unconscious Mind,
Opener of the Inner Eye,
May all that I need to know be revealed to me by your light.

Although obviously much smaller and much closer to us, the disc
of the Full Moon appears from our perspective exactly the same size as
the solar disc, and thus the Sun and the Moon have become symbols of
balance and equality between male and female, day and night, conscious
and unconscious wisdom. The Full Moon illuminates us with a
different light from that of the Sun; it is more subtle, more ambiguous,
more suggestive to the imagination, the light of the unconscious mind.
The world looks different by Moonlight.

This is a good time to view things with a new perspective, to look
around with our inner eye, to connect with our destiny. Questions
which have been baffling us may suddenly find their solutions at this

time, predicaments may be resolved in a new way, anxieties may dissolve when seen in the gentler light of the Moon. However, this may equally be a time of crisis; many people are acutely aware of their mood swings at Full Moon. The term "lunatic" and the legend of the werewolf both take their origins from the known effect of the Moon at this time. It is the high tide of the unconscious, and emotions may overflow.

It is important to take some time out at Full Moon, to be still for a while and listen to her voice, bask in her gentle light and rest in her motherly arms. Burn a fat white candle and incense of Cedar, White Musk or Lily of the Valley. Make yourself beautiful in whatever way best pleases you. Wear something both beautiful and comfortable, allow yourself some "comfort food", play music which calms and uplifts you.

If you can, go out into your garden, into the countryside, up onto high ground, by the sea, a fountain, a river—anywhere where you can experience the full glory of our Heavenly Mother. Open your heart and mind to her light. With your conscious mind, note and give thanks for what you have achieved over the past month, what goals have been reached, what dreams have been realised, what gifts have been received. Then stop thinking, drift off for a while into the unconscious realm, with the silent request that anything you need to know at this point in your life may be revealed to you. You may be surprised at what you bring back with you when you resurface!

Invocation to the Waning Moon

Hail, Grandmother Wise and Serene,
Harvester of Dreams and Guardian of Treasures
Voice of Experience, Loosener of Ties,
Guide of the Lost and Comfort of the Weary!
May I wake to your wisdom and listen to your voice;
I release my burdens and tread lightly in your path.

The waning moon gives us an opportunity each month to let go of what we no longer need, and to gather in and treasure what we have achieved, learned or discovered. This can refer to ideas and opinions, relationships or aspects of relationships, aspects of health, or indeed material possessions. Life is an ever-flowing stream, we learn and we change, and yet so often we persist in clogging the channels of our destiny with emotional and intellectual baggage that we no longer need, repeating past patterns and weighing ourselves down with needless regrets and defences.

The time of the waning moon is an ideal period to give some thought to what we could usefully let go of so that we may travel more lightly along our path. If there is a particular emotional knot that needs undoing, it may be helpful to visualise it in the form of a physical knot that you can then undo, or a stream clogged with leaves and debris which you can clear. Also, reflect upon what you have achieved, and which experiences in your life you really treasure, what you have learned that you wish to keep and use in your future life or pass down to your children. This is a time to walk slowly, to take your time, to sort out your real priorities so that you may know what seeds to sow with the next New Moon.

Dried flowers, shells and stones may beautify your altar, hearth or dressing table at this time of the month; also any gifts of sentimental value that have been given to you by older relatives or friends, whose advice and guidance you have valued. Give thanks for all who have shared the benefit of their experience with you, and for the wisdom of your elders. If you yourself are moving into the latter phases of your life, this is a time to value yourself and your own experience, and to allow yourself to really enjoy your own bright harvest.

Invocation at the Dark of the Moon

Hail, Lady of the Hidden Face,
Mother of Darkness,
Opener of the Depths.
In my darkest hour I reach for your hand;
May my heart return wiser to the light.

The dark of the moon occurs for one night only in the month—the night between waning and new moon, when not even the slimmest crescent, young or old, is visible in the sky. This is the time when we may confront our deepest needs and failures, when we may experience temporarily that inner journey to the Underworld, the "dark night of the soul", which can dissect our personality and render us down to our most basic components. This is the time when we must accept that there are some things in this life which we may never know or understand, and that there are some things which we can do absolutely nothing about.

This is the night of the full stop.

It is good to know that the Moon is still there in the night sky, even though we cannot see her. It is good to know that at those points in our lives where we hardly even know who we are, the Universe still holds us safe in the palm of her hand. Lifetimes and personalities may come and go, but the soul, the essence, is still held safe.

A bare altar or hearth with no candles is best at this time. We may call to mind those we have loved who have passed on, those we may still be grieving for, also those lost opportunities or lost causes which still cause us regret.

Release the grief, the regret, the despair into the arms of the Mother of Darkness. Nothing is lost, only changed. Life is a cycle, and all things return. Have trust—close your eyes but open your heart. Tomorrow is the night of the New Moon.

Tuesday – Invocation to Mars

Hail, Red Warrior,
Lord of Battles and of Anger,
Bringer of Conflict and of Change;
My Soldier and Hero,
My Lover *(or Companion)* and Protector,
I call upon Thee!
Strengthen me in conflict,
Direct me in anger,
Ennoble me in defeat.
May your red cloak shield me from harm and from heartbreak,
May you always find rest in my arms *(or heart)*.

Gods of war and heroes of battle have always strode proud through our myths and legends, inspiring both fear and admiration in the human heart as conflict and courage have shaped our history. We call upon this Deity for courage and protection when challenges arise at home and in the workplace, and conflict with family members, friends, colleagues or complete strangers unsettles our peace of mind and sends the adrenalin racing round our bodies.

We may feel overwhelmed by anger; Mars helps us to control our aggression and channel it constructively. We may feel powerless against injustice or bullying; Mars inspires us to stand up to the aggressor, to claim our rights and state our beliefs. We may feel overwhelmed by fatigue or by money troubles, with children or loved ones to care for and protect; Mars gives us the inner strength we need to persevere. Our conscience may be troubling us; Mars can give us the courage to pick up the phone or put pen to paper, and make that apology. Alternatively we may be feeling hurt, vulnerable, desperately needing care and protection. We may ask the God Mars to place his shield over us, to grant us sanctuary, safety, and the time to rebuild our strength.

Red is his colour; his is the "red planet". Tuesday is his day. Light five red candles and wear something the colour of blood and passion.

Carry with you or lay on your altar or hearth some Holly or Hawthorn. Burn some pine incense or resin. Eat some hot, strong-flavoured food if your digestive system is up to it! On a Tuesday, do something to connect with the hero or heroine within you; even the smallest act of bravery or assertiveness, even the resolution or commitment to make that apology or to stand up and be counted will please the Deity.

Mars brings passion as well as protection, and stirs up desire as well as courage. If you are a woman, you may invoke the God as your lover and hero, recognize and greet him in the eyes of the man you love, or ask that he come to you in human guise, if you are searching for a male lover. If you are a man (or a lesbian), you may invoke him as a comrade and mentor, ask him for help in your quest for love, and request that you appear in his image to your beloved. If you are a gay man, you may like to do both, remembering that the comradeship of the battlefield often overlapped with physical expressions of love between men!

Wednesday – Invocation to Mercury

Hail, Mercury, Bright Messenger of the Gods;
Swift mover,
Quick thinker,
Smooth talker,
Far seer,
I call upon Thee!
Today may I think fast and act quickly,
May I speak articulately and convincingly,
May my intuition be swift and accurate,
May I find myself inspired!
May my ears be open for messages from the gods;
May all that I need to know be revealed to me.

The planet Mercury, closest to the Sun, is also the fastest to complete its orbit; so speed and communication are the keywords here. Thus the god Mercury—Hermes to the Greeks—wings his way between heaven and earth, carrying messages between gods the humans. With his winged heels and helmet, and his "Caduceus", the olive wand with entwined serpents which has become the symbol of healing as well as communication, he is a familiar figure in art and in symbol. His Norse counterpart is Woden, and Wednesday is his day.

You may call upon this Deity for help with all matters related to communication, travel, or the settling of misunderstandings; and for speedy transactions by letter, phone or internet, as well as face to face. You may find Wednesday a good day to back a horse or greyhound; to act on a hunch; to locate a missing object or person; to clear up a misunderstanding, or avoid one by quick thinking and clear speaking ... or conversely, you may wish to cover your tracks, explain your way out of an awkward situation, backtrack, change your mind. Like the quicksilver that bears his name, Mercury is ubiquitous and changeable, and can adapt to any situation!

In accordance with his fickle and changeable nature, there are many colours associated with Mercury: silver, violet, light blue and orange candles can all be used to invoke him; six and eight are his numbers, so you will need a few! Air is his element, Sandalwood or Lavender his incense. He rules the Hazel tree, associated with divination, intuition and flashes of inspiration. A hazel wand or staff was traditionally carried by wizards or wise men who wished to receive and communicate divine wisdom.

Use these associations to catch the attention of this fickle and elusive Deity—he will bless you with his qualities and enable you to take swift advantage of life's opportunities!

Thursday – Invocation to Jupiter

Hail, Sky-Father, Lord of Thunder,
Dealer of the lightning-bolt, I call upon Thee!
Wearer of disguises, springer of surprises,
Destroyer of illusions, I call upon Thee!
Generous Father and giver of gifts,
Law-giver, promise keeper, I call upon Thee!
May I know your blessings, but not perish in your glory;
May you find me deserving of your favour!

Jupiter, Father of the Gods, represents generosity, good sense, prosperity achieved through hard work, success in business, fatherly responsibilities, and family values. His gift is that approach to life that bears his name—joviality. Like most fathers, however, he is perceived by his children as both benevolent and punitive. Remember, this Deity is also Thor, the Norse Thunder God from whom Thursday is named; and in Greek legend he is Zeus, who descended to earth in numerous disguises to seduce unsuspecting maidens—as a swan, a shower of gold, a white bull.

All too often we get the picture of an erring husband and father in the throes of a mid-life crisis, capricious, lustful, easily provoked to anger. But there is consideration behind the mask: one of his conquests in Greek myth, Semele, urged on by agents of his aggrieved wife Hera, demands that her divine lover cast off his disguise. She wants to see him as he really is, in all the glory of the Deity. In vain he warns her that the sight of a God is too much for mortal eyes to bear—she will not take no for an answer, and the full lightning-blast of his glory destroys her mortal body.

So be warned; we may enjoy the blessings of this Deity only if we abide by his rules, and they are there for good reason. We must be honest, generous, and willing to work for our rewards. Any unrealistic illusions may be destroyed by the bolt of his disapproval; but if, like the oak tree that survives the lightning blast with its roots still deep and living in the ground, we are willing to learn by our mistakes and start again, we may be sure that our efforts will be blessed with his fatherly care.

On a Thursday, light four royal blue or purple candles. Burn incense of Cedar. Visit an Oak tree, or better still, a grove of Oaks, sacred to this Deity; meditate upon the tree's qualities of stability, endurance and fatherly protection.

Thursday is a good day to close a deal, to take the initiative in business, to assert your legitimate authority as a parent, teacher or employer; to shoulder your responsibilities cheerfully; to deal with any outstanding legal matters; to visit or think of your father; to be generous with your time or money; to face up to home truths or let go of illusions. It is also a day to enjoy yourself—life is not meant to be one hard slog, the bounty of the Universe and the good things of this world are gifts to be enjoyed. Look on the bright side! Wear purple! Be jovial!

Friday – Invocation to Venus

Hail, Lady of Love and Beauty,
Mother of Mystery, Star of the Sea,
Morning and Evening Star, Virgin and Harlot,
Mistress of Love, I call upon Thee!
Queen of Women, Mystical Rose,
Lady of the Shining Cedar,
Comfort of the Troubled and Hope of the Weary
Flower of the Desert, I call upon Thee!
May my home and my loved ones enjoy your gifts,
And rejoice each day in your blessings.

You may recognise some of the titles used in this invocation to Lady Venus, whose Norse counterpart Freya gives her name to the last day of the working week; many of them are also titles of Isis/Hathor of Egypt, Astarte of Syria, Ishtar of Babylon and Aphrodite of Greece; and some are also to be found in the Litany of the Blessed Virgin Mary, used by the Catholic Church to this day. All of these Goddesses have associations with the beautiful and mysterious planet Venus, which has always held a fascination for astronomers and astrologers alike, changing as it does from a morning to an evening star in the course of its cycle and tracing a pentacle across the night sky in the process.

The planet Venus, appearing low on the horizon, has also been called the Star of the Sea. In Greek legend, Aphrodite is born fully grown from the sea, and first steps onto dry land on the island of Cyprus, where her shrine at Paphos became a centre of pilgrimage in ancient times. She is the Goddess of Love and Beauty, of the irresistible force of sexual passion which is a *sine qua non* of life on Earth. Reflect on how the myth mirrors scientific fact—all life began in the sea, emerging onto dry land to increase and multiply, beautifying the planet in the process.

Thus Venus/Aphrodite is also an aspect of the primordial Mother Goddess, and as such she presides over children and homelife, female friendship and all things feminine, as well as sexual desire. Men and women alike belittle her sphere at their peril—the intellect is no match for Mighty Aphrodite, unstoppable as the tides. She can unsettle the most rational mind and overturn the most dedicated career, as many public figures have found to their cost!

On a Friday, think of ways to honour Lady Venus as you go through the day. Her colours are green, aquamarine and rose pink; the apple, the myrtle, the cedar, the tamarisk, the rose all belong to her, as do the dove, the goose, and cattle. Light a beautiful candle, burn some incense of Rose, Jasmine, Apple or Cedar. Pamper yourself, your beloved, and your children. Spend time on your home and garden, making your surroundings beautiful. Buy or gather fresh flowers for yourself or the one you love. Have a long, relaxing bath, make yourself irresistible. Recognise her in yourself, or in the woman you love. Celebrate her power.

Saturday – Invocation to Saturn

Hail, Wise Grandfather,
Teacher of patience and wisdom,
Slow mover and stirrer of the depths,
Lord of the Cycles of Time, I call upon Thee!
Today with your blessing, may I take my time;
May I walk slowly, may I sit quietly,
May I speak thoughtfully, and listen to advice.
May I endure with patience the turbulence you stir up in me;
Looking back on my life, may I learn its lessons.
I give thanks for all who have taught and inspired me—
May they know my gratitude, and the blessing of the gods!

What goes around comes around, we reap what we sow, and no-one can escape the slow march of Time. These are the lessons of Saturn, grandfather of the gods. Life is a learning curve, and Saturday, his day, usually brings a welcome change of pace after the working week, an opportunity for revision.

Saturn is a slow-moving planet, and takes twenty-eight years to return to the same position in any individual's natal astrological chart. Thus, between the ages of twenty-eight and thirty, and again between fifty-seven and fifty-nine, we experience what astrologers call our "Saturn return". These are important transitions into a new stage of maturity. Old traumas and complications may re-emerge at this time, demanding to be dealt with and finally laid to rest; old habits, relationships or other attachments may be shed quite naturally and painlessly; and old hurts may be healed at last. A new phase of life awaits us at these times—the responsibilities of adulthood, or the new opportunities of "the third age"; some of us live to experience a third Saturn Return in our mid-to-late eighties, when hopefully we may look back in wisdom and serenity at the bright harvest of our life, laughing at our younger selves and marvelling at our own progress!

Saturn is often thought of as rather a sombre Deity—the colour black, the metal lead, the scythe and the hourglass of Old Father Time, are all associated with him. But rest, reflection and change do not have to be burdensome. The Roman Saturnalia, the three days around the Winter Solstice, was a feast of drunken revelry; slaves were relieved of many of their duties, and in some cases waited upon by their masters—role reversal was the order of the day! Everyone made a fool of themselves and no one was held responsible, as the old year died and made way for the new, easing the passage across the symbolic threshold of death and rebirth.

So on a Saturday, by all means have a lie-in, watch the sport on television, and enjoy your Saturday night in whatever way best pleases you! But also take time to reflect and recuperate, letting go of the old week and preparing for the new. Burn three black candles and some incense of myrrh, musk or hemp, and reflect upon life's lessons, giving thanks for what you have achieved and letting go of what you no longer need. Give thanks also for the help you have received along the way, especially from those who have since passed on—honour your elders and your ancestors.

Then put on the little black dress and pearls, or the black leather trousers, and get ready to dance the night away—tomorrow is another day!

Part 2:

Hearth and Home

Blessings for the Home

These blessings may be used at any time. For example, they are particularly appropriate when moving into a new house; you may bless your old home before leaving in thanks for happy times spent there, and as a welcome present for the new owners or tenants; and a blessing in your new home will remove any negative energy that may have collected there, and ensure a happy environment for yourself and your household.

Redecoration, rearrangement of the living space, or preparation for a new arrival to the household are all occasions when these blessings may be appropriate, to ensure that the new energy created by change will be positively charged. You may also wish to bless holiday homes, places where you are staying as a guest, or, with their permission, the houses of your friends. Sometimes it is a nice idea just to renew our appreciation of the home environment with a blessing, or to restore peace in this way after a family argument.

Finally, if you have suffered a break-in or other major disruption to your home, these blessings will help to banish and heal the trauma, restoring a sense of peace and security and making your home feel safe again.

Blessing for the Threshold

May a blessing rest upon this threshold,
The boundary of this home.
May those who cross from without to within be welcomed.
May those who cross from within to without be protected.
May all that is brought from without to within give joy to this home.
May all that is taken from within to without give love to the world.
May no harm pass over this threshold from without to within.
May no ill-feeling pass over this threshold from within to without.
May all who cross this threshold be blessed.
May peace, prosperity and happiness attend this home.

The threshold is very important symbolically, as it marks the boundary between the private and the public sphere. Crossing the threshold into the house, one comes into the realm of the household, where the rules and customs of the family apply. Passing out over the threshold into the outside world, public manners and behaviour apply. Members of the family may come and go across the threshold freely, but guests and strangers must knock at the door and wait to be invited in.

The tradition of the groom carrying the bride over the threshold dates back to Roman times, when it was very important that the mistress of the home should not stumble upon entering her new domain and status, lest this bring bad energy into the marriage!

Blessing for the Hearth

May this hearth be blessed with warmth and with love;
May all who gather round it share in this blessing!
May the gods of this household be honoured here.
May the ancestors of this household be remembered here.
May the elders of this household find contentment here.
May the children of this household find comfort here.
May the familiars[2] of this household find safety here.
May the friends of this household find companionship here.
May the flame of the spirit of this household burn brightly here!

The hearth is the traditional heart of the home, and since in the days before central heating it was the source of warmth for the whole household, it is easy to see why. In simple homes, the hearth would also have served as the kitchen—the modern "heart of the home". The family would gather at the hearth to eat, to keep warm, to bond together, and also traditionally to honour the ancestors. Children were usually nursed at the hearth, and the elderly would have a special place of honour there. The hearthstone was as important as the foundation

---

[2] Family pets, companion animals

stone in the building of a new house, and was often laid with great ceremony and special prayers and blessings. In Ancient Greece, the Goddess of the Hearth was Hestia, who became in Roman religion Vesta, Goddess of Fire, guardian not just of the household but of the entire City of Rome. If the hearth was blessed by the gods and by the ancestors, the household was blessed. If the hearth was cold and unattended, the household was in danger of becoming fragmented.

It is interesting how often in modern homes where the fireplace has been bricked in or is nonexistent, the hearth surround still acts as a focal point, displaying family photos, favourite ornaments, candles or "offerings" of flowers!

Blessing for the Kitchen

May this kitchen be blessed with bountiful stores,
With generous cupboards and cheerful cooks,
With ready water and obliging fire,
With a full kettle and a willing stove,
With inviting smells and comforting sounds,
With happy tempers and good order,
With plentiful helpers and tuneful songs,
With tasty meals and grateful hearts!

The kitchen was not always separate from the living space in the homes of poorer people, but as it has become a separate room in modern industrialised society, it has kept its shared associations with the hearth and is often still described as "the heart of the home". The kitchen is traditionally the domain of the mother. In today's society this may not necessarily be the case, but the associations of food, warmth and inviting smells remain, whoever is doing the cooking!

This is a magical room, where transformation takes place. Raw ingredients are changed into tasty meals here, and in old times it is very likely that medicines, potions and even spells were concocted in the kitchen by the women of the family. Even today, we find ourselves entering a kitchen with feelings of anticipation and excitement—what's for dinner? What's that smell? What's in the biscuit tin? What's in the fridge? The magic lives on.

Blessings for the Bedrooms

There may be several bedrooms in the house, and the same blessing may not be appropriate for all. The marital bedroom, for instance, was traditionally blessed for fertility, fidelity and happiness in the marriage, and this may still be appropriate; but a child's bedroom obviously requires a different emphasis. A spare bedroom, which may be the least occupied room in the house, can acquire a cold, neglected atmosphere; when guests are coming to stay, in addition to changing the bed linen and putting the duster round, you may like to "warm up" the room with a special blessing.

Blessing for the Main Bedroom

May this room and this bed be blessed with a welcome;
May love make a home here, and not depart.
May the worries of the day be left at the door,
And all disagreements be shed with undressing.
May lovemaking be blessed with joy and fertility
And the union of those who love be deepened.[3]
May sleep bring sweet refreshment here,
May dreams bring understanding,
And waking, joy.
May sickness be healed and sorrow soothed,
May sanctuary and safety be assured here.

Blessing for a Child's Room

May *(name)*'s room be blessed with comfort and safety,
And his/her bed with the promise of peaceful slumber.
May no harm enter by day or by night;
May fears and worries find no hiding place here.
May dreams here be sweet,
May thoughts here be happy,

---

[3] These two lines are optional and may be left out if the bed is not shared by a couple.

May hopes and plans be nurtured here,
May loving words be spoken here,
May angels keep watch over *(name)* here.

Blessing for a Guest's Bedroom

May this room and this bed be blessed with a welcome
For all who rest their heads here.
May this be a place of sweet refreshment,
Where trouble and anxiety are left at the door.
May all who sleep here know themselves safe,
The welcome guests of a loving household.
May sleep be peaceful and dreams be sweet
And happy thoughts be left on the pillow!

Blessing for the Study

A study, library or "home office", once the prerogative of the rich, is becoming more common in modern households, often taking the form of an attic conversion. It may still be seen as something of a luxury, but of course it does not have to be a separate room at all, and this blessing may just as appropriately be applied to any corner set aside for reading, study or work:

May this space be blessed with peace and creativity,
With clear thinking and concentration.
May ideas find expression here,
May problems be solved here,
May information be sought and discovered here.
May the fountain of inspiration rise freely in this place
From the well of intuition.
May conscious and unconscious wisdom unite,
That worthwhile work may be done here.

(If a computer or phone forms part of the office equipment, you may like to add the following:)

May this machine be blessed with helpfulness,
With fast and accurate communication,
With freedom from trouble, delay or mischief,
With durability and reliable service!

Blessing for the Bathroom

May this place of ablution be blessed
With cleansing and renewal.
May flowing water bring refreshment here,
Washing away all that soils,
Carrying away all that is unwanted,
Releasing all that is no longer needed,
Refreshing the body and clearing the mind,
Restoring the spirit to face the world!

The bath or shower room, like the kitchen, is a place of transformation. We may enter it weary, dirty and burdened down, and leave refreshed, relaxed, ready to face a new day or to prepare for a good night's sleep. Bathing or washing has always been used as a symbolic ritual, marking the transition from one state or stage of life to another: baptism, ritual baths after childbirth or menstruation, or before entering a sacred place after battle, are all examples of this "larger than life" use of the bathroom; and of course Pontius Pilate's famous hand washing gesture, with which he declared himself not responsible for the execution of Jesus Christ, has become a universal symbol of relieving oneself of responsibility—"I wash my hands of the whole affair". The importance placed by the Romans on bathing and bath houses is well documented, and numerous myths relate the transformative properties of magical baths, the renewal of youth, health or even virginity being among the examples!

Blessing for the Garden

May this garden be blessed by day and by night
With beauty, tranquillity and safety;
With sunshine and shade,
With moonlight and mystery,
With birdsong and laughter and conversation;
With healthy and beautiful trees and flowers,
With fertile soil and lush green grass,
With busy insects and sociable birds,
With fresh sweet air and sufficient rain.
May sorrow and sickness find comfort here,
May discord find resolution and weariness, rest.
May growth of the spirit be nourished here;
May violence and harm be kept far from here.
May gods and ancestors visit here,
May this household find ease and contentment here,
May children and animals play safely here,
May friends and loved ones find a welcome here.

A garden is a blessing in itself; it is a place where the boundary between "outside" and "inside" becomes blurred, where invisible walls maintain the private space of the home whilst opening out that space to become part of the natural world, including the sky, the sun and moon, the energy of trees and plants, birds, butterflies, bees and all the small creatures of the earth in a personal relationship with the home. Even a small balcony can fulfill this wonderful and magical function. This blessing can be used for gardens great or small, or even adapted for a window box.

Blessing for an Altar or Sacred Space

Many homes of differing faiths have an altar or even a special room set aside for prayer or meditation. The altar may be dedicated to a particular Deity or to the ancestors, or it may be for general purposes or adapted for different occasions—the cycle of the seasons, the phases of the Moon, or the days of the week, for example. Households or individuals who follow a particular faith will of course have their own prayers and rituals of dedication, but for those who have no such tradition in place, I would suggest something along the lines of the following:

May this altar/space/room be a place of spiritual power;
May all who approach here with love be blessed.
May those who seek comfort here find consolation.
May those who seek answers here find understanding.
May those who seek direction here be shown their way.

May those who seek a deity here find a true connection.
May those who seek enlightenment here be blessed with progress.
May all who seek peace and safety in this place
Be encircled by loving arms.
May no harm or ill intention find expression here,
May the unworthy remain unaware.[4]

Other Rooms

What about the living room/dining room/conservatory, you may be saying? Well, I am leaving those up to you. I have concentrated upon the most symbolic areas of the house, where particular activities traditionally take place, rather than upon general living space, because I see these as the focal areas which make up a blessing upon the whole house. The hearth, for instance, is usually the focus of the living room, the threshold the focus of the hallway or reception area. If you wish to bless the other rooms in your house with peace, happiness and safety, or with some other particular function, please go ahead and do so—compose your own blessings! I have given you enough to go on!

---

[4] It is a good idea to include an admonition such as this, for it will make your altar or sacred space invisible to those who would ridicule or take offence to it—in other words, they will not see it for what it is.

Part 3:

The Season Round

The Wheel of the Year

The year in ancient times was seen symbolically as a story sequence; the story of the relationship between Father Sun and Mother Earth. This mythical sequence came to be celebrated over eight festivals, combining the four pivotal points of the solar year (the solstices and equinoxes) with the four main festivals of the agricultural year. Thus combined, the celebrations fall roughly at six-weekly intervals. These are the main markers of the Pagan year, as retrieved from ancient times and celebrated by modern Pagans today; and many of them, as you will see, are also celebrated by the Christian Church. The dates given for these festivals are relevant to the Northern Hemisphere—in other parts of the world, the equivalent celebrations would take place on different dates, according to the seasons of the Southern Hemisphere.

These are not only external events; they also tie in with our internal processes. For example, Imbolc, when the light is beginning to quicken and the new growth starts to push through, can be a good time to find the energy to start a new venture. I have included a few suggestions along these lines for each festival, but it is up to you as an individual to look within yourself to discover what each festival means to you at this point in your life.

Winter Solstice

The word "solstice", from the Latin, literally means "the sun stands still". At the Winter Solstice the Sun sets in the southwest after the shortest day, and rises in the southeast after the longest night, at the most southerly point of his yearly journey across the sky. From this point on, the days will grow longer and little by little, the Sun will rise at a more easterly and set at a more westerly point, until at the opposite pole of the year, the Summer Solstice, he reaches his most northerly position in the sky, before moving back again towards the south.

The Winter Solstice occurs on the 21st December, and was celebrated in ancient times as the birth of the new-born Sun, whose promised return each year secured the revival of vegetation, the fertility of Mother Earth and the survival of crops, animals and humans. The newborn Sun Deity was known by many names, and in the case of the Roman cult of Mithras, his birth was only celebrated in earnest once the visible proof of his return in the form of lengthening hours of sunlight became evident, three days after the Solstice on December 25th. Thus it was only logical that when Christianity became the official religion of Rome, the celebration of Christ's birth was also given this date; and the Solstice has been celebrated in the Christian world under this guise ever since.

This blessing may be used at any time between 20th December and 1st January, when the Roman god Janus, with his two faces looking back to the past the forward to the future, brings our modern calendar into line with the solar year.

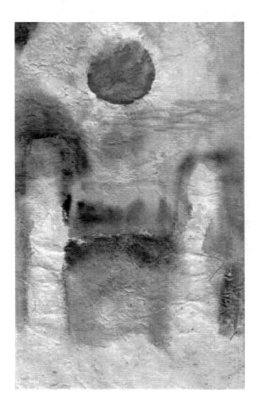

A Blessing at the Winter Solstice

We ask a blessing at the threshold,
At the moment of standing still;
Between the death of the old Sun,
And the birth of the new.
At the turn of the wheel,
At the end and the beginning,
May we be blessed.
May the wisdom and love of our ancestors
Guide us across the threshold
To greet the new-born Sun.
May we carry with us the past year's treasures:
All we have learned,
All we have loved,
All we have achieved,
All that has brought happiness—
These we bring into the bright new year,
Leaving the rest behind.
May we grow in wisdom, health and happiness,
As the days grow longer,
As the light grows stronger,
As the wheel swings upward,
As the new year progresses.
May we walk with confidence,
Without looking back,
In the footprints of our destiny,
In the path of our future.

Imbolc

Imbolc, also known in ancient times as Brigid, is celebrated on 2nd February, when we greet the first signs of Spring. The Celtic goddess Brigid is a Maiden aspect of the Great Goddess, and a triple goddess of poetry, healing and smithcraft. She was particularly popular in Ireland, where she continues to be honoured by the Christian Church under the guise of St Bridget. The title "Fair Maid of February" also applied to the snowdrop, the earliest spring flower, referring to her as the protectress of the young girl who celebrates her changing body at puberty; but in the Catholic Church the feast of Candlemas is celebrated on this date in honour of another Virgin Goddess.

Candlemas is the Feast of the Purification of the Blessed Virgin Mary—"purification" referring to the ancient Jewish rite of renewal after recovery from childbirth. A Jewish mother would normally return to sexual activity after this rite, thus the theme of renewal and fertility applies to both Christian and Pagan celebrations on this date.

Imbolc is a fire festival—white candles are lit outside the church at Candlemas and carried inside, bringing "new fire" into the sanctuary. In Pagan celebrations, bonfires are lit, processions are held often headed by a young girl dressed in white, the ploughing of fields and the sowing of seeds are blessed, and the earliest signs of Spring, the keeping of the Earth's promise, are greeted with joy, relief and gratitude.

This blessing may be used at this time to encourage us to put some of those New Year's resolutions into action, start some new projects, and realise some hopes and dreams.

A Blessing at Imbolc (Candlemas)

We ask a blessing in the morning of the year,
When Mother Earth stretches, yawns and stirs
At the hesitant caress of the shy young Sun.
Prodded from beneath by eager shoots,
Ploughed from above into furrow and ridge,
She wakes, she rises, smoothing her hair,
And dresses in white and green—
In snowflake, snowdrop and lamb's fleece,
In shoot and blade and birdsong;
The Mother herself reborn, renewed,
Opens her hands in blessing.
And so, as we sow the seeds of hope,
As we tend the shoots of inspiration,
As we dance in the Spring with fire and with drum,
Singing of joyful expectation,
May the Fair Maid of February bless us all!

Spring Equinox

The Spring Equinox falls around 20th-21st March, varying slightly from year to year. For this one day, the hours of darkness and light are equal, and from that day onwards the days will be longer than the nights until we reach the Summer Solstice. This is the beginning of the astrological year, when the Sun enters the sign of Aries the Ram, and Spring starts in earnest. Trees begin to come into leaf, birds of all species are busy with their nests, and many animals give birth to their young at this time.

The Celtic Goddess of Fertility, Eostre, whose name is linked to the word "oestrogen", was naturally celebrated at this time of year; her symbol was the egg, her sacred animal the hare—and these, along with her name, have been carried over to the Christian festival of Easter, which also celebrates a promise of new life. Other fertility Goddesses such as Astarte and Cybele were also honoured at the Spring Equinox.

The Equinox is a time of balance, a time of reassurance that all is as is should be. The promise is fulfilled, the earth becomes beautiful and fertile once more, and new life appears. The Sun God is a child no more, but a young man and a lover. He woos the Maiden Goddess who herself has become fertile and desirable, and their joy in each other blesses all the children of Mother Earth; may we have time and awareness each Spring to share in it!

A Blessing at the Spring Equinox

We ask a blessing as the year comes of age,
As the young Sun comes into his strength
And completes his initiation,
Wrestling with darkness, equal to equal
And tipping the balance, seizing victory
And running with it, exultant, to greet his beloved!
See how his lady bedecks herself
With lily, daffodil and furled new leaf,
How she shakes her skirts and tosses her hair,
Her laughter ringing across hill and valley,
swooping and trilling, lowing and bleating,
Rejoicing with her love!
Now is the time of rising sap,
Of fertile juices, busy nests and leaping hares;
With bird and beast, with tree and flower,
May we be blessed with rejuvenation!

Beltane

Beltane is celebrated on May 1st—still a national holiday in Britain—with processions, garlands of Hawthorn (also known as "May"), the choosing of a May Queen, and dances round the May Pole.

Many of us took part in these festival celebrations as children, unconsciously celebrating our Pagan roots.

The Maypole, traditionally made of Ash, can be seen as a phallic symbol, representing the virility of the God as he celebrates his union with the Goddess. It is decked with ribbons and crowned with Hawthorn, which before the calendar was revised in 1752 would have been in bloom at the beginning of May, rather than at the end of the month as now. These red and white flowers are said to exude a female sexual aroma. It is an old superstition that it is unlucky to bring Hawthorn garlands into the house; they were strictly for outdoors. Dances around the Maypole were originally fertility dances, performed at first separately by young women and young men, but progressing to the selection of a partner and the more intimate dancing of courting couples. As the afternoon wore on with feasting, singing and plenty of beer to quench the thirst, Nature would be guaranteed to take care of the evening's activities!

Today only a male fertility dance survives—the Morris Dances, which still traditionally involve the use of stout Ashen poles. May Fairs all around Britain still kick off with a Morris Dance; although some Morrises prefer to wait until the first New Moon in May, honouring the old lunar calendar. One of the proposed origins of the term "Morris Men" is "Mary's Men"—Mary being seen as an aspect of the Goddess— and indeed in the Catholic Church, May is traditionally Mary's Month. Many Catholic households still set up a "May Altar" in the home, dedicated to the Blessed Virgin, at this time of year. Thus the paradox embodied by the Maiden Goddess, who was saluted as both "Virgin and Harlot", is celebrated unknowingly in the modern world.

Finally, it is interesting to note that if we are following the myth of the solar year in order, the Goddess is already pregnant at the time of her May wedding with the young God who was conceived at the Spring Equinox and will be born at the Winter Solstice. Thus Nature, when all is said and done, always takes precedence over social convention!

A Blessing at Beltane (May Day)

We ask a blessing as the year is crowned
In the merry month of May,
When apple and cherry blossom strew the path
And horse-chestnut lines the processional route
With flowery candles for the Queen of the May
As she rides, hawthorn-crowned, to her wedding.
We ask a blessing as the maypole is crowned,
The rising Ash with the fragrant Hawthorn,
The lusty god awaiting his bride,
Feted with ribbons and dance and song.
We revel in the blessings of love and desire,
As the heart dances to the drumbeat of life;
With the Lord and the Lady, with wine and with song,
In happy union may we be blessed!

Midsummer

The Summer Solstice occurs between 20th and 21st June each year. Here the Sun reaches his most northerly point in the sky, rising in the northeast and setting in the northwest; his longest journey across the sky from our point of view, and the longest day of the year. Midsummer celebrations in the old days took place from dawn to dusk, and even today thousands flock to ancient sites such as Stonehenge to watch the Sun rise on the longest day at the very point marked out by our ancestors. It is a day of feasting and jubilation, but tinged with sadness—from this point the days will grow shorter, and nights longer, and the long descent into winter begins. The point of triumph is also the point of no return—until, of course, the Sun is re-born at the Winter solstice, and the wheel swings upward once again.

However, the midpoint of the solar year is only the beginning of Summer as we experience it in the Northern Hemisphere. Throughout the months of July, August and most of September we continue to experience the long hot days, the beauty and of course the harvest that is the legacy of the love story between Father Sun and Mother Earth. Even as he prepares to leave us, he blesses us, giving his remaining strength to the crops of grain and fruit which will sustain his children through the winter months. Now is the time for us to give appreciation to our own achievements, great and small, and resolve to enjoy them, turning dreams into reality as the year matures.

A Blessing at the Summer Solstice

We ask a blessing on the longest day,
As the sun achieves his glory;
At the highest point of the wheel,
The pinnacle, the climax,
In the breathless moment may we be blessed.
This is our darling's perfect day;
Here he rests in the arms of his love,
And here, having touched perfection, he dies,
Lets go, and begins the long descent,
Trailing his clouds of glory.
Tomorrow begins the long goodbye,
As the harvest, his legacy, ripens;
But today we adore him from dawn till dusk
And surrender ourselves to his love.
May all our achievements be blessed today,
All our efforts rewarded;
May our dearest wishes, our secret hopes,
Our midsummer dreams come true.

Lammas

Lammas falls on 2nd August, when the first crops of wheat, corn and barley are ready for harvesting. It is a time for celebrating the grain, the staff of life, the gift of the dying Sun to his human children. The word "Lammas" comes from "Loaf Mass", the thanksgiving of the Christian Church for the first harvest of the year. The alternative name for this festival, "Lughnasadh", is Irish Gaelic and refers to the wake of the Celtic Sun God Lugh who gives his life to the grain. It was at this festival that our ancestors would share the harvest loaf as the body of the God, and drink red wine or berry juice to symbolise his blood, giving thanks for the sacrifice that enabled the agricultural community to survive and to store for the coming winter. Thus another parallel between the old religion and Christianity becomes evident at this time.

There are many local folk customs by which people continue to honour the Lord of the Harvest in the manner of their ancestors, and these vary from one area to the next; but a common theme involves saving the final sheaf of the harvest—in the old days often decked with ribbons and garlands and carried in procession from the field to the barn with great rejoicing, and finally made into a "corn dolly", which was kept for a year as a sign of the promise of the next harvest.

Lammas is a time for us to bring in our own personal harvest, great or small, making that final effort to complete tasks or projects left undone, or carry through those resolutions made earlier in the year. Then is the time for thanksgiving, and for taking time off from all our hard work to enjoy the full glory of Summer, while the days are still longer than the nights and the Earth is still warm from the Sun's embrace.

A Blessing at Lammas (Lughnnasadh)

We ask a blessing at the harvest of the grain,
At the Sun's wake, as we share his gifts,
Bringing home the first-fruits of his bounty.
See how he bequeaths his gold to the fields,
The blue of his sky to the cornflowers,
His life's blood sprinkled in poppies across the land.
Now the air hangs heavy and sweet like honey,
And the trees stand stately, in full leaf,
As Mother Earth shakes bounty from her lap.
The shouts of holiday children rejoice the ear,
And Summer sighs in our hearts, full to the brim.
The seed of light that was hidden in the earth
Has fathered the grain, the staff of life!
With the sun-kissed fields, with the golden sheaves,
With harvest and harvester, may we be blessed!

Autumnal Equinox

The Autumnal Equinox falls between 22nd and 23rd September, when night and day once again balance each other equally, when the final harvest both of grain and of fruit is gathered, and schools and churches all over the country celebrate Harvest Festival. It is traditionally a time of thanksgiving for Earth's bounty; communities would celebrate both in thanksgiving and in order to ensure that the gods would continue to bless them with a sufficiency of food for the year ahead. In the times when there was little or no imported food, and what one ate during the winter depended on what one had grown or gathered at this time, the thanksgiving for a good harvest was heartfelt indeed!

Once the Equinox had passed, the shorter, colder days would very quickly bring home the approach of Winter, and it was important to prepare a good larder if one was to survive in comfort. As well as the preservation of fruit, nuts and vegetables, any surplus cattle would be slaughtered and the meat dried and salted to add to the Winter supplies.

Having made Mother Earth fertile and provided for his children, the Sun "sets sail" in the West and prepares to depart, ready to return again as a newborn child at the Winter Solstice. This is indeed a time for counting and harvesting our blessings, for looking back on the year and taking stock, preserving those achievements and experiences we wish to keep and giving thanks for lessons learned, gifts received and dreams fulfilled. It is also a time for making the most of any last minute opportunities, living in the moment and enjoying the "season of mists and mellow fruitfulness" to the full.

A Blessing at the Autumn Equinox

We ask a blessing as the year matures,
When fruit hangs ripe and heavy on the bough
And Mother Earth prepares a harvest supper,
Calling us all to share in her largesse.
With bird and beast,
With spinner and gatherer,
With hoarder and scavenger
Let us join the feast!
Now has the Sun achieved full fatherhood,
His light now gentle, his embrace still warm.
This is his final gift, his farewell feast—
At this day's end he kisses the horizon
And sets sail on his long voyage back to birth,
Letting the nights close in.
Now is the time for us to count our blessings.
As we bid farewell to Summer with grateful hearts.
As we gather and prepare for the coming Winter,
Let us pause awhile in the lap of bountiful Autumn,
At the turn of the Sun-tide, and know ourselves truly blessed.

Samhain

The old Celtic festival of Samhain (pronounced "Sow-in") falls on 31st October and marked the end of the old Celtic year and the beginning of the new. The veil between this world and the next is thought to be lifted at this time, and special attention was paid to one's ancestors. A place would be laid at the table for a loved one recently departed, and they were invited, if they wished, to join the New Year's feast. This was a time when people could communicate with the departed, asking for advice, reaffirming love, or maybe hoping to heal old hurts and misunderstandings which had not been dealt with in life.

It is easy to see how the modern festival of Halloween emerged from this tradition. Even though it is primarily seen in popular culture as a festival for children, the celebration of ghosts, magic and "wicked witches" triggers our unconscious link with the "otherworld", the supernatural and the next life at this time of year, when the nights grow ever longer and the landscape bleak and bare. Death and disappearance are all around us, and we seek the hope of renewal, and the assurance that this is not the end, that the cycle goes on and life returns.

In the Christian Church, the festivals of All Souls (All Hallows Eve!) and All Saints are celebrated on 31st October and 1st November, once again affirming that this is the time of year to pray for and celebrate those who have passed into the next life. The Pagan and Christian celebrations, once of one mind, have sadly become opposed in modern life as some Christians condemn the celebration of Halloween as having links with so-called "black magic".

Many of us like to make some offering or communication with our departed loved ones at Samhain. The apple and the pomegranate, symbolising life and death, are traditional fruits to leave out as offerings; in addition, it is useful to write out a list of the names of those one wishes to remember, together with any important thoughts, messages or blessings. Then we in turn will receive the blessings and reassurance we need, with the knowledge that love, like the soul, never dies.

A Blessing at Samhain (Halloween)

We ask a blessing as the year begins to close,
As the last leaves shrivel and fall
And wood smoke drifts on the evening air.
Now is the time when bird and bee fall silent,
Listening for other voices;
Earth withdraws into herself,
And our thoughts also turn inwards,
To contemplate the soul.
Now, if we listen, we may hear our ancestors
Whispering to us—
Words of wisdom, warning or comfort
Fall on the inner ear.
From all that we have harvested, learned and enjoyed this year
Let us make an offering for our departed;
Let us tell them of our love, our regrets, our gratitude,
Ask for their blessings
And bless them in return:
May they be well. May they be happy.
May they be there to greet us when we too pass on.

Part 4:

Invocations for Special Occasions

Blessings and Invocations for Special Occasions

The following blessings and invocations can be used to celebrate those key transitional points which mark the different phases of our individual lives: the birth of a baby, the bestowing of a name, the transition from childhood to adulthood, the commitment to sharing one's life with a partner, the acceptance and celebration of old age, and finally the passing of the human spirit from the body at the end of life.

It is usual to call in the powers of the four elements (air, fire, water and earth) when creating sacred space. The following Invocation, for example, was written for a naming ceremony which took place on a fine day in ancient woodland. Each of the elements, air fire earth and water, are invoked in the corresponding direction.

Invocation for a Naming Ceremony

Powers of the East, Element Air, we ask that you bless our child *(name)*. May his/her thoughts be clear and his/her visions strong. May the gift of inspiration be his/hers. May the winds of change guide him/her. May the beginning of his/her journey through life be blessed.

Powers of the South, Element Fire, we ask that you bless our child *(name)*. May s/he know the heat of passion, the strength of courage, the power to meet challenges and to dare. May the fire of life warm him/her as s/he continues on his/her travels.

Powers of the West, Element Water, we ask that you bless our child *(name)*. May the oceans hold safe his/her deepest emotions, may s/he feel the turning of the tides and flow with them. May s/he value and use his/her intuition. May s/he know and honour the power of twilight and the time of shadows.

Powers of the North, element Earth, we ask that you bless our child *(name)*. May the earth support him/her on his/her journey and heal his/her pains and hurts. May s/he honour the silences and stillness of caves and dark places. May s/he be sustained and nourished.

(This is the final blessing for the same ceremony; again all the elements are incorporated.)

Blessing for a Naming Ceremony

Welcome to the earth that is your home.
May you breathe fresh air,
Enjoy the warmth of the sun upon you,
Be refreshed by the cool waters.
May the land protect you as you protect the land.

Blessing for a New Mother

Blessed are those who pass on the torch of life!
Blessed are mothers, who carry in their bodies
The miracle which sparked the Universe!
Blessed are you, who have brought life to birth.
May happiness attend your experience of motherhood;
May the love which binds you to your child
Be unconditional and everlasting, as Nature intended.
May the love which you receive from your child,
Bring lasting delight to your heart.
May you be blessed with strength of body and spirit,
With patience and understanding,
With gentleness and wisdom,
With courage and fortitude for the task ahead;
May you always find support and encouragement at hand,
May fatigue, ill health and despair be kept far from you,
May your faith and your love be greatly rewarded,
May your child bring you nothing but joy.

Blessing for a New Father

Blessed are those who pass on the torch of life!
Blessed are fathers, who protect and serve
The miracle which sparked the Universe!
Blessed are you, who have ignited the spark
And welcomed this new life into the world.
May happiness attend your experience of fatherhood;
May the love which you feel for your newborn child
Become an everlasting bond between you.
May the love which you receive from your child
Bind you to lifelong devotion, come what may.
May you be blessed with strength of body and spirit
To care for and protect this mother and child.
May you be blessed with patience and understanding
To teach and encourage this child as s/he grows.
May you be blessed with gentleness and wisdom,
To guide and comfort this child through life's turmoil.
May you be blessed with courage and fortitude,
To support this family through difficult times.
May your fatherly devotion be greatly rewarded;
May your child bring you nothing but joy.

Not all parents are the biological mothers or fathers of the child
whom they love and care for. This blessing can be used for anyone who
becomes a step-parent, an adoptive parent, a co-parent, foster-parent or
guardian, at any stage in the life of their child.

Blessing for a New Parent or Guardian

Blessed are those who guard and nurture life;
Blessed are you, to whom a child has been given.
May you fulfill this trust faithfully and with joy;
May the love which binds you to this child

Be unconditional and everlasting;
May the love which you receive from this child
Bring lasting delight to your heart.
May you be blessed with strength of body and spirit,
With courage and fortitude for the task ahead.
May you be blessed with patience and understanding
To teach and encourage this child as s/he grows.
May you be blessed with gentleness and wisdom
To comfort and guide this child through life's turmoil.
May you always find support and encouragement at hand,
May your love and devotion be greatly rewarded,
May your child bring you nothing but joy.

Blessings Upon Entering Adult Life

In Western society we are unique in having no acknowledged "rites of passage" for young people with which to mark the transition from childhood to adult life. In other parts of the world these are seen as very important, and often involve painful and demanding tests of endurance, resulting in physical scars to remind the young man or woman of their new status. Girls at least have the milestone of the menarche, the onset of menstruation, to demonstrate that they are changing from a child into a woman; but this is rarely celebrated properly, even though it is one of the fundamental "women's mysteries". For boys, the boundary between child and man is less dramatically marked; Jewish boys celebrate their bar mitzvah at the age of twelve or thirteen, when they may or may not have embarked upon the physical changes of puberty; but the blessing below may be most appropriately given following some physical sign of maturity, e.g. the voice breaking. As with the menarche, there is no fixed age—it is an individual journey.

Menarche Blessing for a Young Woman

We welcome you at the threshold of womanhood
To the sacred cycle of blood and life.
May you be blessed as the power awakens within you.
May you grow in beauty of body and mind,
Increasing in confidence, strength and skill
To outride the storms of puberty.
May you come into your womanly power
And use it wisely, and with kindness.
May your growth to maturity bring you nothing but joy;
May the Goddess smile from your eyes.

Blessing for a Young Man

We welcome you at the threshold of manhood;
May you be blessed as you come into your strength.
May you grow in beauty of body and mind,
Increasing in confidence, courage and skill
To outride the storms of puberty.
May neither anger nor fear overwhelm you;
May you willingly shoulder responsibility
And be the protector of those who love you.
May you win admiration and respect,
May the God shine out from your countenance.

The following is a final blessing from a commitment ceremony, where two people come together to honour and bless their relationship in public so it can be witnessed by friends and family. These kinds of ceremonies have been especially important to same-sex couples who have traditionally been excluded from expressing their love in this way within the mainstream religions. This blessing includes a quality from each of the elements.

Blessing for a Commitment Ceremony

As your love keeps flourishing
May you continue to learn from each other
May you inspire each other
May your feelings rise from the depth of your being
May you offer a helping hand in times of difficulty.

The next poem was written for a particular couple at their ceremony of commitment by a close friend, Asphodel Long (to whom this book is dedicated), who was not well enough to attend.

Asphodel's Poem for a Commitment Ceremony

Blessed be the hands that clasp together
Blessed be the lips that touch!
Blessed be the voices that sing together
Like the blackbird's song in the joy of the day,
Like the mermaid's song at night,
Repeating their magic chants
To a fiery moon on the dark green ocean;
And the Summer trees murmur their chorus
And the poppies and orchids abound,
Giving life to the bees, your guardians;
Let sky dance!

For some of us, the hours we spend in paid employment accounts for a large portion of our time. It is also an area of our lives that can be difficult, and where we may feel we have little control. It is important to remember in the modern world that if we act responsibly and with integrity, we are a success in the eyes of the Universe. There are things we can do at work to remind ourselves that we are on a sacred journey—placing a special object on our desk, for example a stone or a shell. If we have a job that keeps us on the move, we can keep it in a pocket. The following words, with any appropriate adaptations and changes, can be said before leaving home for work.

Blessing for Work

May I go about my work with kindness and respect for others;
May my actions be thoughtful and my words honest.
May I walk my path carefully with spirit;
May I value myself and my contribution,
And know my best endeavours are always good enough.
I ask for clarity of vision and an unclouded judgement,
And that I may return home empowered and fulfilled.

In modern industrialised societies with youth-oriented cultures, aging is often seen as a negative process. This has not always been the case, however, and indeed is still not in some cultures today. It has often been the older woman who was seen as influential within a society, possessing wisdom and being respected for her decision-making powers.

Some women today are looking to reclaim this part of their lives as an important and empowering time, and wish to mark the time that they start to identify as an older woman, as Crone. There is no generally agreed time as to when this should be. Some people take reaching the age of 50, when they may have stopped menstruating, as a threshold. However, especially given the average life expectancy in our society, this is relatively young. Others see their second Saturn Return as marking the occasion—when Saturn is in the same position as in the natal chart for the second time in our lives, between 58 and 59 years. Saturn is the planet associated with consolidation, and it can involve quite a stormy time as we are confronted with some of the difficult aspects of our life. The age of 70 can also seen as a time when a woman reaches cronehood. Personally, we favour the last two.

Below is a welcome, probably spoken by an older woman who is herself a crone, which can be used as part of a ritual.

A Welcome to Cronehood

You who have heard the many secrets borne on the wind,
Who have been engulfed by the flames of passion and courage,
Who have drowned in the oceans of the mother to re-emerge,
Who have been both lover and protector of the land,
We welcome you.
May owl bless you with wisdom,
May fox bless you with cunning,
May dolphin bless you with kindness,
May snake bless you with renewal,
Timeless woman, we honour and welcome you

This blessing may be helpful in marking retirement, the end of
one's working career. For men in particular, this is sometimes a
traumatic time as many men tend to define themselves by their work,
and feel that they have lost their function and meaning in life when
they no longer have the structure of the working day. It was therefore
written with men in mind, but of course could equally be applicable to
the working woman.

A Welcome to Retirement

Welcome, weary soldier,
Veteran of battles lost and won;
You who have been buffeted by the winds of fortune,
Who have been scalded in the fires of passion,
Whose cheeks have been grooved by many tears,
Whose body as known both ecstasy and pain—
Welcome to this threshold.
Here you may lay down your burdens,
Letting go of what you no longer need.

Gather together your real treasures—
Achievements, experience, wisdom and love—
And carry them with you into this new phase of your life.
Here may you find honour, respect, reward;
There is time and space now to put right past wrongs.
May you learn new skills and discover new happiness,
Be a teacher to the young and a guide to the lost,
As you place yourself at the helm of your destiny
And seek out your own true harbour.

When someone dies, we may want to send a blessing to help them on their way from this life into the next. Whatever we may believe about the afterlife, and whatever the beliefs of the deceased may have been, the following blessing can be used as a template and adapted to make it more personal and relevant to those involved. It can be used either in public, at a funeral, or in private as you light a candle at home in honour of the one who has passed on.

A Blessing at the End of Life

May you go in peace, and arrive with joy;
May all the love you have given and received go with you;
May the gratitude of all those you have helped
Stand against any debts that you carry from this life;
May the Divine embrace receive you.
Go home; be well; be happy.

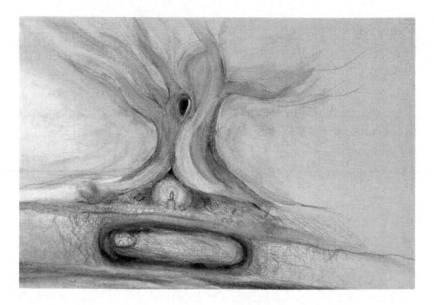

Finally, we may like to ask a blessing for ourselves, to help us deal with the transition that takes place in a relationship when someone dear to us dies. The blessing below was recited at the funeral of a dear friend; it is hoped that these words can bring comfort and hope to those who are grieving.

Final Blessing at Asphodel's Funeral

May the power of air keep our memories and visions bright and clear;
May the power of fire inspire us and give us courage;
May the power of water let our emotions flow and change;
May the power of earth support us as we continue on our journey.

Part 5:

Gods and Spirits

Invocations to Deities

Within what is generally called Paganism, there are many different Deities, and diversity is something to be celebrated rather than a cause of conflict. This is called polytheism and is fundamentally different to some mainstream religions that are monotheistic and only acknowledge one God. The Deities selected here are deliberately taken from outside the classical pantheon referred to in the section on the days of the week.

The following are invocations or prayers to a small sample of the many Gods and Goddesses from around the world. It is hoped that the reader may be inspired to create their own to honour the qualities of a particular deity at an appropriate time. There may be a particular culture that someone identifies with and deities from this part of the world will have a special meaning to them. The first three invocations were written during a second Saturn return and are about recognising the value of difficult times in our lives.

Anyone with respectful intentions may approach and invoke a Deity. If you feel a link with a particular God or Goddess, you need only look within your heart to find the appropriate salutations; although of course it is always helpful to do a bit of research and try to find out whether any particular offices and titles were attributed to that Deity in ancient times.

The Scorpion

This was written in honour of Selket, an Egyptian Goddess, who is often depicted as a woman with a scorpion's head. She is a Goddess of magic as well as a symbol of motherhood and nurse to the king. It was also believed that she led the dead into the afterlife.

They say the sting is in the tail;
They say we should avoid it, pull free,
But I say take me there, let me feel it,
Let the agony storm through me,
Healing me, cleansing me,
Leaving me peaceful and reconciled.[5]

In Honour of Yemaya

Yemaya is a West African Goddess. She is sometimes described as the Queen of Mothers. She is the Mother of the sea and as such the mother of all life.

Great and wondrous Mother,
From you the springs well up,
From you the rivers run free,
From you the oceans burst forth!
We drown in your presence,
We give birth in you honour.
You heal us, you join us,
You love us, disorientate and overwhelm us;
You command that we return to you.
Yemaya, ever-living through all times and all dimensions,
We lose ourselves in you so that we may become who we truly are.

---

[5] Apparently the sting of the scorpion also contains the antidote.

To Oya

Oya is another West African Goddess. She is wild and has been described as a "mother of chaos". She is associated with weather, and all the elements—earth, air, fire and water.

The winds of change are on their way—
Earthquakes threaten to tear apart the ground on which I stand,
Lightening is ready to strike,
The sea to surge up!
And I stand in the middle of this
And wait for you to absorb and fill me
So I can walk along my path with power.

To Bride

Brigit, Bridget or Bride is an early Irish Goddess who became incorporated into the Christian religion and was made a saint. She is particularly honoured at Imbolc, the beginning of February, when the light begins to quicken as the Sun returns.

Oh Bright One, our ever living flame,
Lighting the fires of new beginnings,
Warming the Earth, awakening the slumbering,
Infusing us with imagination and inspiration!
Bride, matron of smith craft,
Bride, matron of midwives,
We call you and honour you at this time!

To Sulis

Sulis is associated with both the sun and water. In Britain there is a shrine to her at Bath, where the water from a hot spring is said to have healing properties. The Romans "merged" her with their own goddess, Minerva, and sometimes she is referred to as Sulis Minerva. When we visit somewhere special, we can remember to honour the local deity or spirit of the place.

Oh great healing goddess,
Poised on the edge of elements,
Binding together both water and fire;
We immerse ourselves in your presence
To be warmed by your heat
And cleansed by your waters.
For these gifts we give thanks.

To Epona

Epona is a horse goddess and her name gave us the word "pony". The horse was an important totem animal in Britain, and it is still not generally accepted to eat horseflesh in this country. Epona has been seen as protector of horses and those who ride them; she was honoured by the Roman cavalry. She could also take the form of rushing water and has been revered for her healing abilities. This prayer to Epona focuses on her role as protector of horses, and can be said if there are any concerns about attacks on horses, or about their well being generally.

Ancient goddess, divine mare
Born of man and horse!
We ask for your protection—
That you surround your foals
And those who care for them

With healing and safety.
May those who seek to harm your creatures
Face your wrath, oh mother of horses!

To Kuan Yin

Kuan Yin is a Chinese Goddess found within the Buddhist tradition, although it is likely that she is older than this and was originally known as Kwannon, a Japanese goddess frequently portrayed riding on a dolphin. She is known as The Mother of Compassion and has captured the imagination and hearts of many Westerners living in societies that are lacking this emotion.

Great Mother of Compassion
Who cares for all her children,
We know you hear our prayers
And understand our pain and sorrows.
We call on you in our time of need,
And ask that you carry us in your arms
As you ride your sacred dolphin
Through the watery realm of the mother
So we may be healed and restored.

Invocation to Sekhmet

This Invocation to the Egyptian lion-headed Goddess, Sekhmet, a Goddess of battles and retribution and a strong protectress, was written by a twelve-year-old girl, Pip Raven. Pip has been drawn to Sekhmet since the age of three, when she first began to ask questions about the Egyptian Gods and Goddesses. If you find it difficult, as an adult, to feel or establish a link with a Deity, it may be helpful to look back to your childhood years and remember any "imaginary" relationships with deities or angels—it may be that the link already exists, but has been buried under social or religious conditioning.

Sekhmet, Powerful One,
We of the human race bend our knee to you
In acknowledgement of thy superiority
One of greatness and beauty that none may describe
Beloved one who guides us on to the light
Guarder of sleeping ones
Protector of those in need of help
Awakener to those unseeing
Divinity of war and caller to battle
Revenger upon those deserving
Bringer of independence, courage and understanding

Mother of images
Winner of all warriors
Mighty one of lions
Creator
We call to thee in search of guidance.

To The Horned One

This next piece is in honour of the Horned God who resides in woods and forests. His image was perverted by Christianity, and he became associated with the Devil who is often portrayed with horns. However, horns are a symbol of his wildness. While he is free to be wild, this does not include cruelty. The Horned God is sometimes known as Herne, sometimes Cernunnos. He is associated with the dark and the Winter. He is a dying God; he dies so the life force can return after the Winter Solstice when the Sun is reborn. He is an interesting and refreshing image of masculinity in today's modern society.

Lord of the forests and dark places,
We ask that we may enter your sacred realm
That we may hear your music and song,
That we may honour all creatures of this place
And listen to the wisdom of the whispering trees,
And to the voices deep inside us.
As we follow you in your antlered form
We continue on our own transformative journey
And give thanks for this time.

To The Holly King

Another aspect of this Winter Deity is the Holly King. The Holly with its sharp prickles and bright red berries symbolises courage and protection, and is often brought into the house over the Winter Solstice to protect the newborn Sun during those vulnerable first days until Twelfth Night. Sometimes the Holly King is depicted wrestling with the Oak King, Lord of Midsummer, at both the Solstices; at the Summer Solstice the Holly is victorious, and at the Winter Solstice, the Oak King triumphs and the Holly King dies as the new year begins. Alternatively, as here, he dies in the embrace of Winter at the Solstice, and it is his sacrifice that is celebrated with wreaths and garlands of Holly at this time of year.

We honour you, Lord of Darkness.
Dancing and singing with mirth and merriment
As you meet with the Hag of Midwinter,
Losing yourself in the Divine Embrace
You lay yourself down upon the land.
Annihilated by the power of her kiss
You have turned the wheel.

Sacrificial Kings

Around the Mediterranean and in the Near East in ancient times, vegetation and corn gods were honoured in accordance with the yearly cycle. They are all dying-and-rising gods, and their often elaborate myths have this in common: they are loved by an aspect of the Mother Goddess as both son and husband, they are cut down in their prime, and the Goddess, after a period of inconsolable mourning, follows her beloved to the place of death and brings him back to the world of the living.

Obviously this mythical sequence mirrors the cycle of the year, and the death and resurrection rituals were celebrated either at the Spring Equinox for renewed vegetation, or during the Summer at the grain harvest. The gods thus honoured included Dumuzi, Thammuz, Atthis, Osiris, Adonis—and yes, there are parallels with Jesus Christ, not forgetting our own John Barleycorn! The Goddesses associated with them were Ishtar, Astarte, Cybele, Isis, Aphrodite, and Mother Mary. The women of the community would weep and mourn and sing the lament of the Goddess for her lost beloved for a specified period of time, before his revival was celebrated with processions, joy and feasting. Some of these laments have come down to us almost in complete version, and they are very beautiful and moving.

This is a modern Lament to the Syrian Corn God Thammuz, who was associated with both Ishtar and Astarte. He was ritually mourned during the month of "Thammuz"—July—in ancient Syria. It is essentially a woman's lament for beloved young man whom she thinks she has lost irretrievably, but she comes to the understanding that it is change and not loss that she is mourning, and thus finds comfort and even cause for celebration. The most obvious modern application of this is when a son grows up and/or leaves home.

Of course, in Greek legend the Goddess Ceres, giver of corn and vegetation, mourns for her daughter Persephone who had been abducted and taken down to the Underworld, withholding both Springtime and Harvest until her beloved daughter is returned to her; so the parents of a daughter may find these words equally applicable.

A Lament For Thammuz

Where have you gone, my darling, my beloved,
Golden and beautiful as the summer hills?
When I think of you gone, my heart is a reaped field,
Barren and scorched, stony, devoid of shelter,
No longer a haven or home for any creature.
When I think of you gone, my heart is a yawning chasm,
A bottomless well, fed by the waters of Chaos.

Where will I find you now that the field is empty?
How will I know you now, so utterly changed?
The corn is gone from the field; my heart will follow.
The grain is threshed from the corn; my heart will follow.
The grain is ground by the mill; my heart will follow.
It becomes the bread of life—my heart has found you!

And so I will mourn no longer, my beloved ,
Lest the corn grow stagnant and ruined in the field,
And the field remain unploughed, and never nurture
The seed that will bring the young green corn again.
Go with my blessing, and return in freedom!
Change with my blessing, for my love stays with you.

Invocations to Animals

Traditionally humans have sought out animals and their powers in times of need. This idea has become live again in industrialised societies with the introduction of New Age practices such as neo-shamanism. What follows are a few examples of how we may call upon a particular species of animal to help us. It goes without saying that when we ask for help we need to use that help wisely as well as give thanks for it, and of course the reader can create their own invocation to an animal that has special meaning to them.

Mouse

People sometimes mistakenly overlook some of the smaller creatures, seeing them as less powerful. I believe one of the great abilities of the mouse, for example, is that it can go to places that are inaccessible to larger animals. It can find a way through in times of difficulty where others cannot.

Small creature going unnoticed and unseen,
To whom stalks of corn are mighty plants;
You who can see the minute details of the Earth,
You who can find almost invisible pathways—
Please lend me your power
And help me find a way through!

Fox

Sometimes we find ourselves in situations where we need to be on our guard; where we need to use our cunning to achieve the best result and keep ourselves safe rather than jumping in with both feet first.

Waiting, listening, motionless for a while,
Surveying the land with your watchful eyes;
Advancing with stealth,
Your footsteps make no sound
As you move ahead unnoticed,
Using all of the senses,
Alert to the possibility of danger.
Lend us your power in times of need!

Frog

Frogs (and toads) have traditionally been associated with magic and transformation. This fascinating creature changes from tadpole to frog, and fairy tales are full of stories of people who get turned into frogs and back again. This kind of animal power can be called upon when we need to adapt to new situations and challenges.

Great magician,
Creature of transformation,
Knower of nature's magical ways!
Shifter and changer,
Touched by the phases of the moon,
Crossing the boundary of land and water—
We adapt our being
To all of our changes.

Badger

Badgers are the oldest mammals in Britain that are still with us today. They were known to our ancient ancestors. I believe this beautiful and mysterious animal is a guardian of old knowledge and keeper of deep secrets. Badger may be invoked when we are serious about understanding the folklore and traditions of the land.

Creature of the night and twilight time,
Holder of the keys to the wisdom of the land,
Teller of mysteries, past and present,
Oldest of kin and friend of our ancestors;
Deeply connected to the energy of earth,
You know the power of roots and the power of herbs.
Elusive you remain in the realm of shadows;
May I honour your presence and learn from your ways!

Owl

When we especially need to act wisely the owl might spring to mind. This bird is a creature of the night, and is often associated with wisdom within British culture. Owls are renowned for their hearing abilities and are able to locate small creatures in the darkness. They may be the guardians of knowledge that can be hard to seek out.

Old wise one, graceful silent flyer
Awake while we mortals slumber;
At home in your shadowy realm
You know the secrets of the night
And the mysteries of the dark.
Hearing and seeing where we can not,
May you guide me in my visions
And lead me to the truth that I seek!

About the Authors and Illustrator

Rose Alba is a modern Pagan dedicated to the service of the Goddess Astarte. She gained a degree in Theology (BD Hons) at London University before turning her attention to Classical and Neo-Paganism, which she has been studying for many years now. She is the author of two novels under the name of Rohase Piercy: *My Dearest Holmes* and *The Coward Does It With a Kiss* . Both of these books are available through Amazon.com.

After many years as a housewife and mother, she has taken up writing again. Some of the material used in this book was originally written in the course of her studies, and some has been specially written for the designated section of the book. All of the Invocations and Blessings are used by Rose and her family in their everyday lives, and she hopes that her explanations and suggestions are encouraging and accessible for the reader. Rose Alba lives in Brighton, England, with her husband and two teenage daughters, two cats, one dog and a shed full of racing pigeons.

Penny Barham first became involved in the Women's Spirituality Movement during the 1980s, and gained a certificate in Feminist Theology from Lampeter University in 1996. Also in the 1990s, she started working with the Scandinavian Center for Shamanic Studies, and was part of an ongoing group which the Centre facilitated.

She lives in Brighton and is a qualified reflexologist. She is also a shamanic practitioner and works with neo-shamanic healing techniques. She has been a celebrant at funeral, commitment and naming ceremonies, and she is also the executor of the late Asphodel Long's literary estate.

Over the past few years she has published a number of articles, including *On the Threshold of Power*, published in *Spirit Talk* issue 3, 1996 (looks at the potential of women as they reach their menopause); *Baubo and Women's Sexuality*, published in *Goddessing Regenerated* issue 7, 1997 (considers images of the healing power of older women's sexuality in myth); *The Dance of the Deer*, published in *Goddessing Regenerated* issue 9, 1998 (explores the existence of deer worship in ancient Britain); and *Black Madonnas*, published in the Spring issue of *Feminist Theology* (Sheffield Academic Press, 2003).

Angela Davis is a painter and shamanic practitioner living in rural Herefordshire. She exhibits her paintings internationally and facilitates creative art workshops. Her website can be found here:

http://www.angelasarthealing.co.uk/healing-art.html

The cover art and the interior pictures are all her work, listed as follows:

> Dreaming (cover)
> Waning Moon p. 9
> Chalice Bearer p. 18
> Kitchen Window p. 27
> Personal Altar p. 32
> Returning Sun p. 37
> Golden Harvest p. 45
> Parent and Child p. 55
> By Water p. 62
> Kuan Yin p. 70

Power Place p. 72
Fox p. 77
White Owl p. 79